Ludwig van Beethoven

COMPLETE PIANO SONATAS

Edited by

HEINRICH SCHENKER

with a new introduction by

CARL SCHACHTER

IN TWO VOLUMES

VOLUME II

(Nos. 16 - 32)

DOVER PUBLICATIONS, INC.

NEW YORK

This Dover edition, first published in 1975, is an unabridged and corrected republication of *L. van Beethoven / Klaviersonaten / Nach den Autographen und Erstdrucken rekonstruiert von Heinrich Schenker*, originally published in four volumes by Universal-Edition A. G., Vienna and Leipzig, ca. 1923.

The footnotes have been translated, and Schenker's preface retranslated, specially for the present edition, which also includes a new introduction by Carl Schachter.

The publisher is grateful to Miss Marie Powers for lending copies of the original for reproduction. A number of corrections have been introduced tacitly into the text of the present edition.

International Standard Book Number: 0-486-23135-6
Library of Congress Catalog Card Number: 74-83473

Manufactured in the United States of America
Dover Publications, Inc.
31 East 2nd Street, Mineola, N.Y. 11501

Contents

Volume II

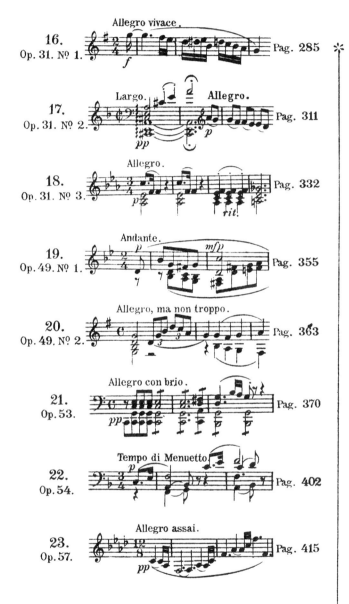
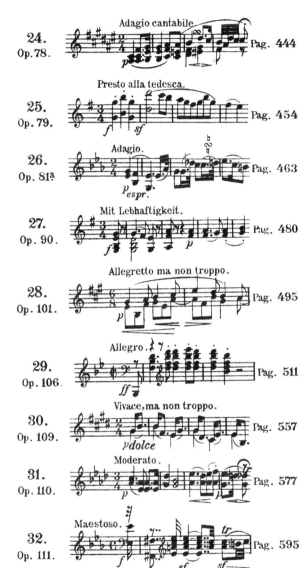

SONATE.

Op.31. No 1.

L. van Beethoven.
(1770–1827.)

1) The fingering in italics is Beethoven's.

Adagio grazioso.

1) In the original edition (Cappi, Simrock) *g–b–d–f.*

1) The trills in mm. 99 & 100
with Nachschlag.

1) In contrast to the original edition, many editions give *g* as the first 8th note, as in m. 28; but only *b* is justified in this passage.

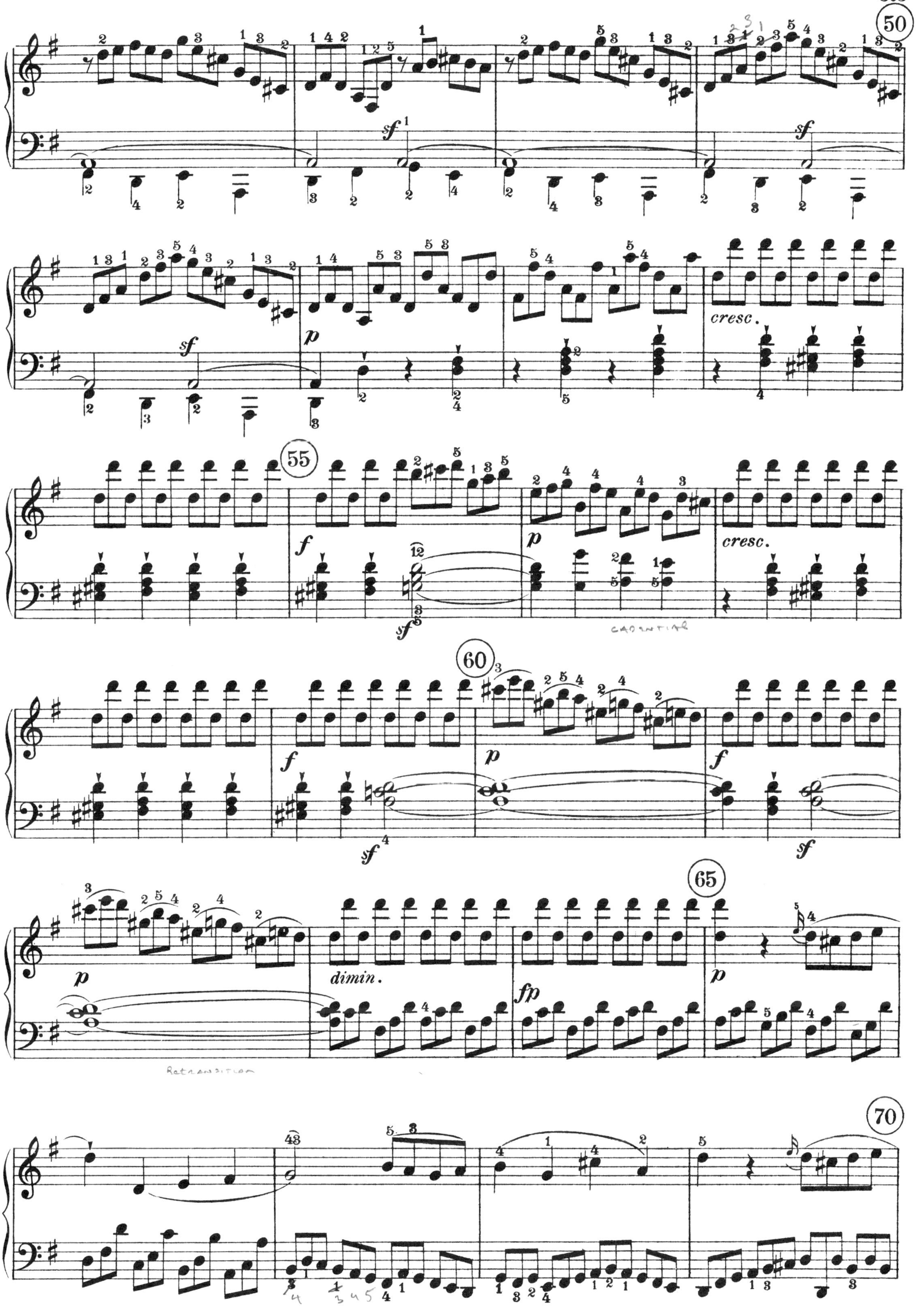
50
cresc.
55
cresc.
60
65
dimin.
70

SONATE.

Op. 31. No. 2.

1) The fingering in italics and the pedal indications are Beethoven's.

1) Thus in the original edition; it
   can also be executed:

1) See the execution in m. 10.

1) With Nachschlag. 2) With Nachschlag.

Allegretto.

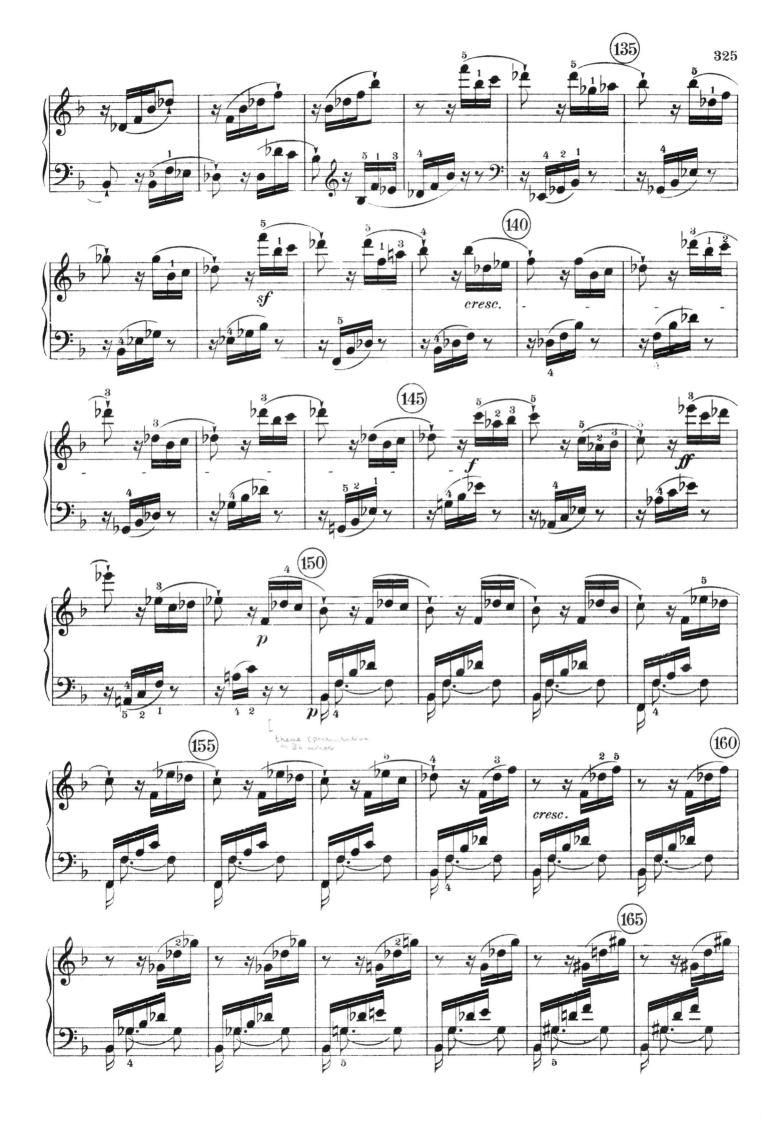

SONATE.

Op. 31, № 3.

1) With Nachschlag.

338

340

SCHERZO.
Allegretto vivace.

1) Beethoven could not carry the preceding motif into the higher octave since his piano had no g^3 or ab^3.

sempre staccato

MENUETTO.
Moderato e grazioso.

1) With Nachschlag.

SONATE.

Op. 49, № 1.

1) 2) With Nachschlag.

1) Thus:

RONDO.
Allegro.

Sonate.

Op.49, No 2.

1) The original edition (Bureau d'Arts et d'Industrie, Vienna) lacks dynamic marks completely; the basic dynamics were supplied by the editor.

1) Thus: ♪. The oldest notation for all appoggiaturas, ♪, which Beethoven curiously uses here (cf. the *prallender Doppelschlag* [turn with appoggiatura and short trill] in Op. 54), leaves the decision between long or short appoggiatura to the performer. Here an expressive short appoggiatura is intended.

1) With Nachschlag.

Tempo di Menuetto.

SONATE.
Op. 53.
Dem Grafen von Waldstein gewidmet.

Allegro con brio.

1) The fingering in italics and the pedal indications are Beethoven's.

1) The original edition shows: [musical example] Both the b^3 and the d^3 are engraving errors; if Beethoven had intended the d^3, he would have had to make it the first note of the measure (2nd 16th).

INTRODUZIONE.
Adagio molto.

RONDO.

Allegretto moderato.

Attacca subito il Rondo:

sempre pp

1) The intention of Beethoven's long pedals, which take no account of dissonant passing chords or mixtures, is a spiritual, almost transcendental, binding-together of larger groups, which his instrument also favored (cf. Op. 31, No. 2, first movement, mm. 143–148 & 153–158). On modern instruments one may try to achieve this effect by half-pedaling at the passing harmonies (mm. 3, 7, 11, 15, etc.), a kind of legatissimo of the pedal, comparable to legato playing in general. 2) The pp at G_1 serves to identify the opening of the motif. 3) Thus in the original edition; some later ones give g^3 in place of f^3.

1) The first 16th note is·detached to identify the opening of the motif. 2) Trill starting with the upper note in 32nds. 3) As Beethoven indicates at mm. 490 ff., the trill starting with the upper note is to be played uninterruptedly in 32nds; the fingering given makes this easy to execute.

1) The two 8th-rests in place of a quarter-rest, and the ✳ directly below the fourth 8th-beat, are based on the original edition.

1) Usual simplification.

1) In the autograph Beethoven wrote: "Those who have too much difficulty with the trill where it occurs along with the Theme, can use the following simplification: or, depending upon the extent of their powers, can double it by playing two of these sextolets to every quarter note in the bass. At any rate it is not important if this trill comes to lose some of its usual speed."

SONATE.
Op. 54.

In tempo d'un Menuetto.

22.

1) The *tr* sign in m. 16 and the ℘ in mm. 18, 20 & 24 (thus in the original edition, Bureau des Arts, Vienna) actually seem to call for the following execution: ⟨notation⟩. This differs from the simple turn and the *prallender Doppelschlag* (turn with appoggiatura and short trill) primarily in the isolation of the 1st note (cf. the *geschnellter Doppelschlag* [rapid 5-note turn beginning with the main note]); in any case it is imperative to shorten the last 16th note to a 32nd (see *Beitrag zur Ornamentik*, Universal-Edition 812, pp. 50ff.).

1) The three 8th notes joined by a slur, although they belong to the upper voice (and are thus logically shown in the text), can also be played by the l. h.; likewise in mm. 54 & 56.

1) Short appoggiatura.

1) Here 6 = 2 x 3.

1) The lower note introducing the trill can also be played by the l. h.; likewise in the following mm., 134 & 135.

2) Perhaps: etc. Thus, on the whole fermata measure 2 x 3 quarters.

1) With Nachschlag.

1) The original edition prints an *A* in place of the *B♭♭*.

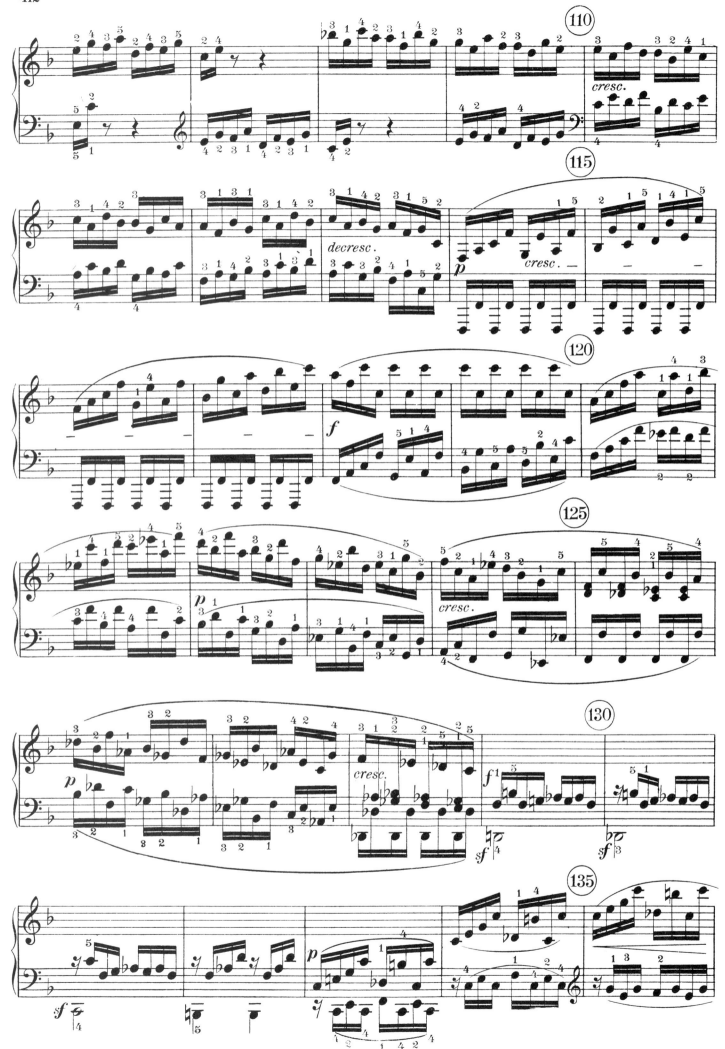

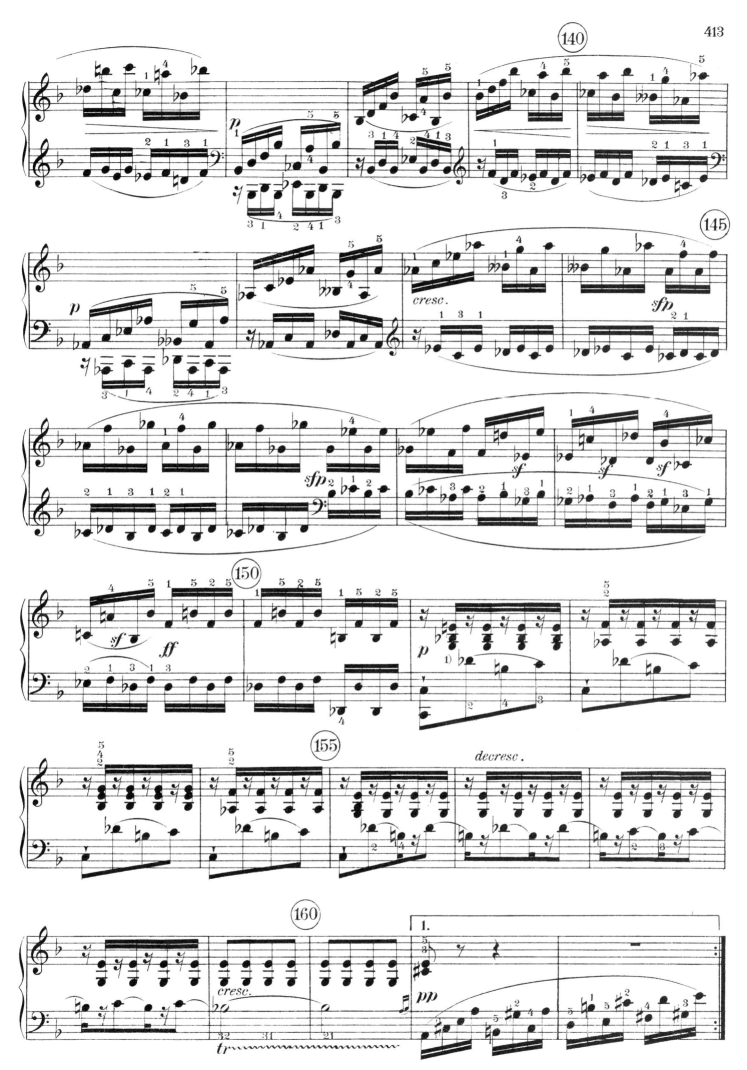

1) The l. h. over the r. h.

SONATE.

Op. 57.

Dem Grafen Franz von Brunswick gewidmet.

Allegro assai.

23.

1) The pedal indications are Beethoven's. 2) Trill from below, with an anticipation (c^2) inserted into the Nachschlag:

The shortest execution perhaps thus:

. 3) In the autograph and original edition (Bureau des Arts, Vienna) the trill has no addition to it;

here one might add g^2 as a short appoggiatura. 4) Only the original grouping of the arpeggio fits the musical meaning.

1) etc. 2) Also thus: 3) As at 2).

closing group
periodic

continuation

1) In the autograph and original edition, e^2 instead of $f\flat^2$.

418

1) In this measure and in m. 160 only the written-out simple Nachschlag is permitted, not the form in m. 156 or 162.

1) In the autograph and original edition, no addition to the trill.   2) Cf. the footnote to m. 45.

1) In mm. 204–205 & 206–207 the 16th-note figure on the first and second quarter-beats—over the long halfnotes in the l. h.—represents 3 × 4 sixteenths; with the beginning of the motif in the l. h., each group of six sixteenths forms a unit. Therefore, to reproduce on the last two quarter-beats the figuration of the first two, as printed in many editions, contradicts the musical meaning.

1) This exact reproduction of the autograph and original edition from m. 227 to m. 234 excludes a distribution of the music between both hands. The fingering supplied within parentheses is a suggested simplification through use of the l. h.

430

1) Here, as in mm. 60, 64 & 72, the use of the thumb on the upper keys, too, makes the execution easier and more supple.

1) The tie clearly in the autograph.

1) In the autograph there is a natural sign before the *D* in mm. 291 & 295.

SONATE.

Op. 78.

Der Gräfin Therese von Brunswick gewidmet.

Componiert im Oktober 1809.

1) The fingering in italics and the pedal indications are Beethoven's.

2) Here, in contrast to Op. 54 (cf. 1st movement, mm. 18, 20 & 24), a true *prallender Doppelschlag* is wanted:

3) In the autograph and original edition (Breitkopf & Härtel) the l. h. has *g* instead of *f* ✕ in this measure and the next.

1) See footnote to m. 17. 2) In the autograph and original edition the l. h. has *c* instead of *b♯*.

1) It is unacceptable here to repeat the f♯ of the second quarter-beat, since the third g^1–e^1 has motivic significance; see the thirds e^2–c♯^{2}, d^2–b^1 and b^2–g♯^{2} in the following measures.

450

1) The l. h. over the r. h.

1) This measure, in a way, amounts to four 8ths: C♯, c♯, c♯¹ and the 8th-rest.

Sonate.

Op. 79.

Presto alla tedesca.

1) The pedal indications are Beethoven's. 2) Thus in the original edition (Breitkopf & Härtel); the difference between the harmonic anticipations in this measure and in mm. 56 & 127 is intentional.

1) See footnote to m. 5.
2) Here still *forte*, in contrast to the *piano* group in mm. 66–74; mm. 83–89 stand in the same *forte–piano* contrast to mm. 90–98.

1) See footnote to m. 5. 2) The 3 notes of the turn fall in the 2nd quarter-beat.

1) Long appoggiatura, thus equal to a 16th.

SONATE.
Op. 81ª

Das Lebewohl.

Bei der Abreise S. K. Hoheit des verehrten Erzherzogs Rudolph. Wien, am 21. Mai 1809.✳

Adagio.

26.

attacca subito l'Allegro.

Allegro.

✳) "On the departure of H. M. the revered Archduke Rudolph. Vienna, May 21, 1809." (The French entered Vienna in 1809.) In opposition to Beethoven's specific instructions, the original edition bears a title he complained of several times: "Sonate caractéristique: Les adieux, l'absence, et le retour" (The Farewell, The Absence, The Return—Das Lebewohl, Abwesenheit, Wiedersehen).

1) The fingering in italics and the pedal indications are Beethoven's.

1) In the autograph there is a *p* here too, in place of the erased ➤

1) The slur here follows the autograph and the original edition in its difference from mm. 23 & 24.

1) Here the slur is once more like mm. 23 & 24, again on the basis of the autograph and original edition.

1) *d²* in the l. h. chord according to the autograph.

Abwesenheit.
Andante espressivo.
In gehender Bewegung, doch mit Ausdruck.

1) Execute the ornament (*prallender Doppelschlag*) before the second 8th-beat.
2) Execute the ornament on the fourth 32nd-beat.
3) Beethoven was obviously thinking of a *prallender Doppelschlag* ornamented in trill-like fashion:

Wiedersehen.

Vivacissimamente.
Im lebhaftesten Zeitmaasse.

Im Januar 1810.

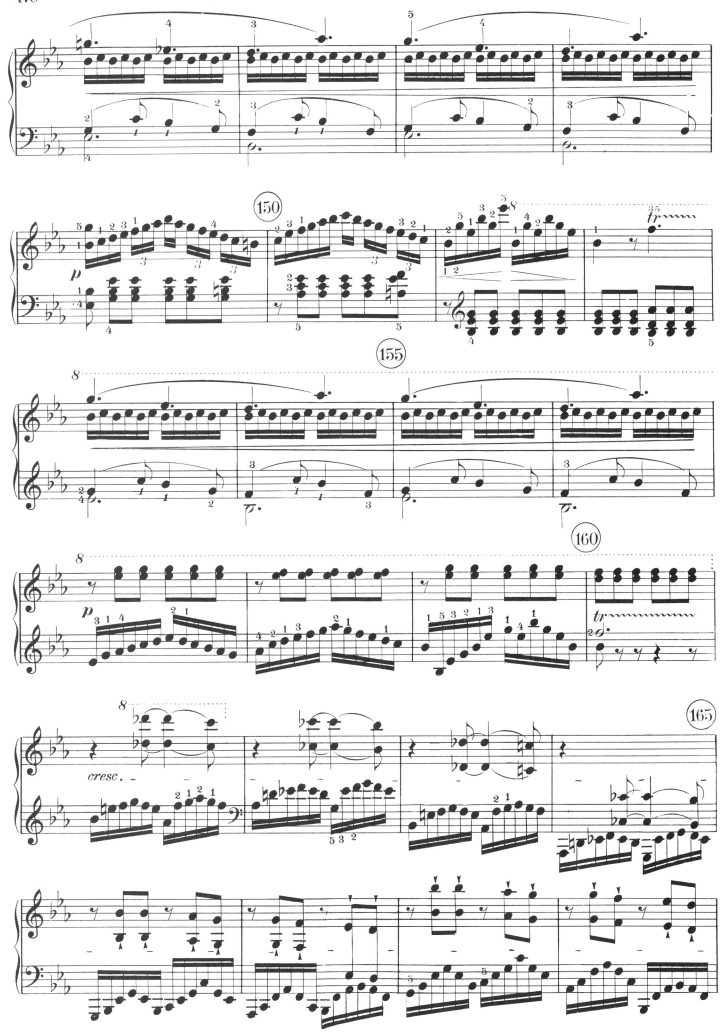

SONATE.

Op. 90.

Dem Grafen Moritz von Lichnowsky gewidmet.

⑤ Componiert im August 1814.

Mit Lebhaftigkeit und durchaus mit Empfindung und Ausdruck.*

27.

*) Lively, with feeling and expression throughout.

1) The l. h. below the r. h.

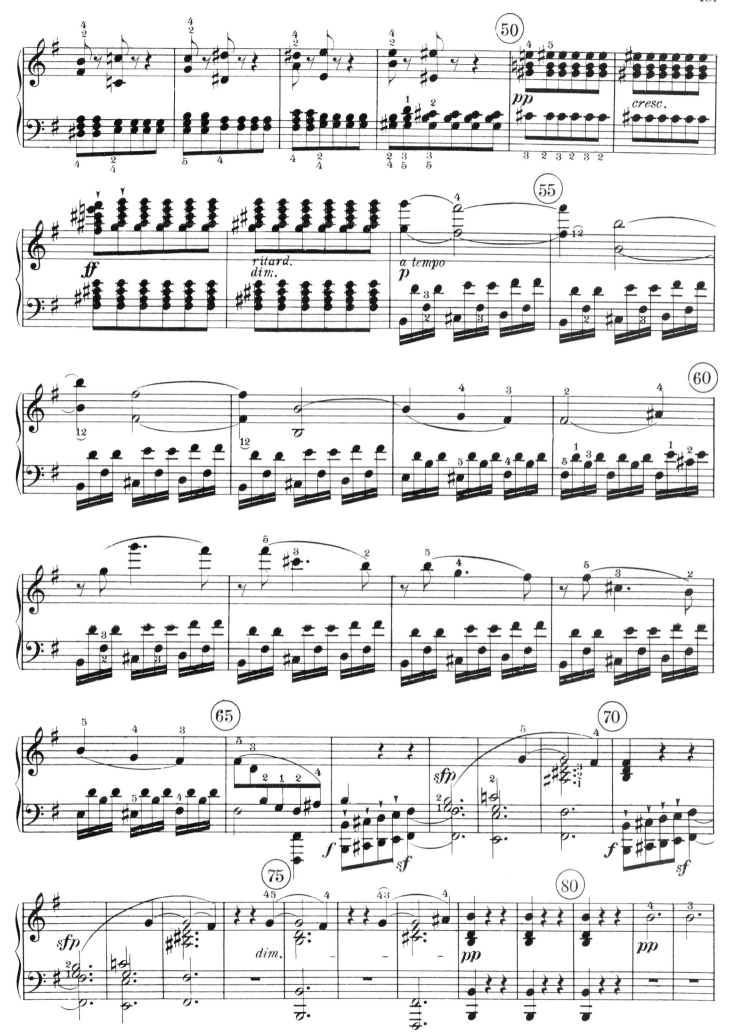

1) The l. h. below the r. h.

1) In the original edition (Steiner, Vienna) this chord lacks the *a*[1].
2) In the original edition the first 8th note has no octave.

Nicht zu geschwind und sehr singbar vorzutragen.*

*) To be played not too fast and very songfully.

1) The repetition of this group of measures, in mm. 17–24, is characterized not only by the octave reinforcement but also by the variant of the neighboring note g♯ in m. 21.

1) In the original edition the e^2 is a quarter note, not an 8th. 2) In the original edition the $f\#^1$ is a quarter note, not an 8th.

1) See footnote to m. 13.

492

1) In the original edition the *B* in the bass is a quarter note. 2) In the original edition this chord has *f♯²*, not *d♯²* as in recent editions.

1) & 2) In the original edition the 2 *b*'s are not tied between measures.

3) The failure to recognize the 2nd imitation ($g\#^1$–$f\#^1$–e^2–e^2) between mm. 284 & 285 is the cause of the incorrect slurs in all editions. In the original edition the execution of the correct slur is faulty.

SONATE.

Der Freiin Dorothea Ertmann gewidmet.

L. van Beethoven, Op. 101.
1816, im Monat November.

Etwas lebhaft und mit der innigsten Empfindung.*
Allegretto ma non troppo.

*) Somewhat lively and with deepest feeling.

1) The fingering in italics and the pedal indications are Beethoven's.

Lebhaft. Marschmäßig.
Vivace alla Marcia.

Langsam und sehnsuchtsvoll.

Adagio, ma non troppo, con affetto.

502

Zeitmaß des ersten Stückes.

Tempo del primo pezzo: tutto il cembalo ma piano

Alle Saiten.

presto.

Geschwind, doch nicht zu sehr, und mit Entschlossenheit.*

Allegro.

*) Fast, but not excessively, and with determination.

508

SONATE.

Op. 106.

Dem Erzherzog Rudolph gewidmet.

29.
(Sonate für das Hammerclavier.)

1) The metronome marks, the pedal indications and the fingering in italics are Beethoven's.

1) The r. h. over the l. h.   2) The l. h. over the r. h.   3) The r. h. over the l. h.

1) In the original edition (Artaria, Vienna) there is no middle voice.
2) A ♯ in front of the *d* in the bass, as in the original edition, is impossible for reasons of voice leading.

1) The trill must not be interrupted; cf. Op. 53, last movement, mm. 485 ff.

1) The r. h. over the l. h.

516

1) If this notation of the original edition reflects the autograph correctly, it shows how Beethoven performed this measure.

1) The voice leading in mm. 222–227, i.e. the 5–6 alternation $g''–g\sharp''–a''–a''–b\flat''$, calls for an *a* in this highly contested passage; it can only be by oversight that there is no ♮ in front of the *a* in the original edition.

1) The r. h. over the l. h.   2) The l. h. over the r. h.   3) The l. h. over the r. h.

1) This trill may also be terminated:

SCHERZO.
Assai vivace. (♩.=80.)

1) It cannot be determined whether Beethoven forgot this b♮—it is lacking in the original edition—or did not want it.

1) Thus in the original edition.
The sense of the arpeggiation is: (cf. the crossing of the hands in the 1st movement, m. 54); recent editions give the
incorrect reading: etc. 2) The l. h. over the r. h.

1) Thus in the original edition for:

1) The original edition lacks the ties.

Per la misura si conta nel largo sempre quattro semicrome, cio è ♪ ♪ ♪ ♪

1) In the course of the fugue it becomes clear that the trill Nachschlag is not always essential for Beethoven; in fact, it cannot always be executed. The instances of Nachschlag which do not appear in the original edition are placed within parentheses.

1) In mm. 48, 49, 50 & 51 the Nachschlag must be played broadly enough so that there is no gap before the third quarter-beat.

1) The trill in the l. h. may be postponed to the beginning of m. 113.
2) This notation, printed here for the 1st time since the original edition, clearly shows Beethoven's performance practice: it was more important for him to have the r. h. play the thematic leaps of a tenth (in contrary motion, b♭–g) than to have the trill continue in one hand. Thus, the significance of the trill once more becomes secondary.

1) The r. h. over the l. h.

1) In mm. 174–179 a trill without Nachschlag.

1) Here and in the following measures the trill may end at the fourth 8th-beat.

1) but the simple *Pralltriller* (inverted mordent) is also sufficient.

1) In mm. 308–317 a trill without Nachschlag.

1) This notation of the original edition indicates the mode of execution.

SONATE.
Op.109.
Fräulein Maximiliane Brentano gewidmet.

*) The fingering in italics and the pedal indications are Beethoven's.

559

Gesangvoll, mit innigster Empfindung.
Andante molto cantabile ed espressivo.

VAR. I.
molto espressivo.

VAR. II.
leggiermente.

567

VAR. III.
allegro vivace.

VAR. IV.

etwas langsamer, als das Thema.
un poco meno andante ciò è un poco più adagio come il tema.

tempo primo del tema.

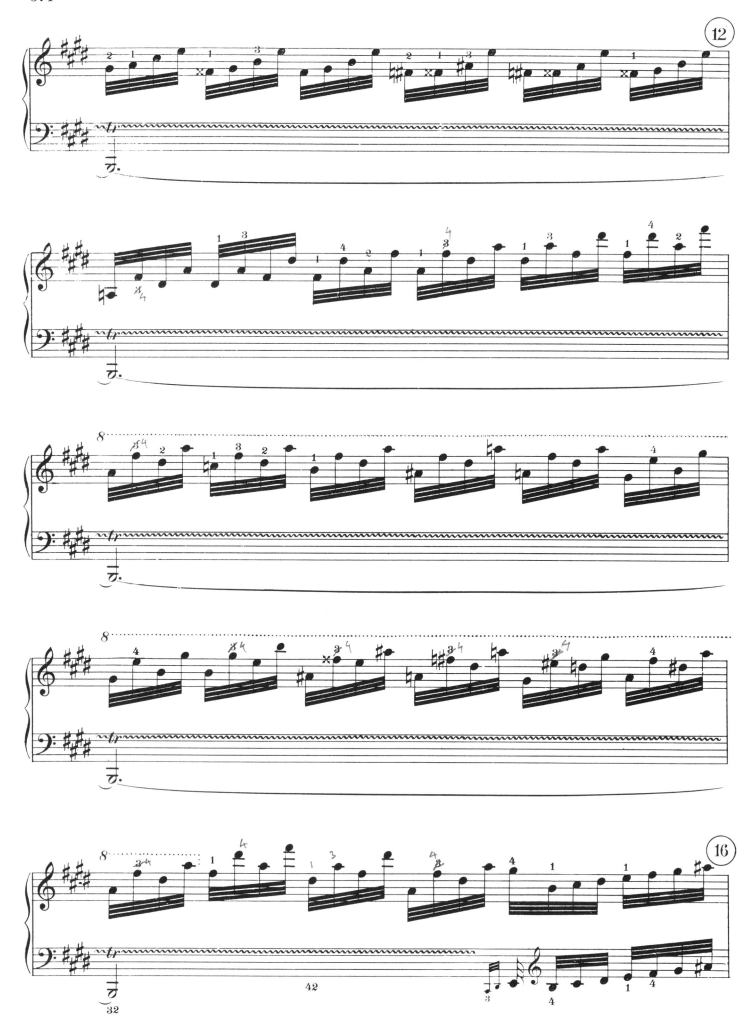

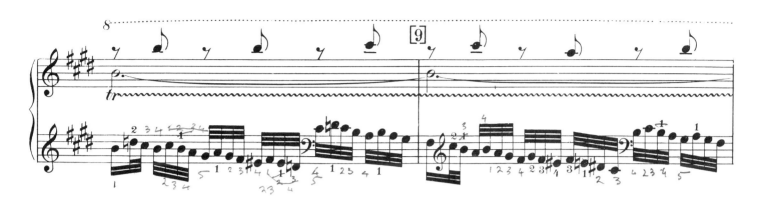

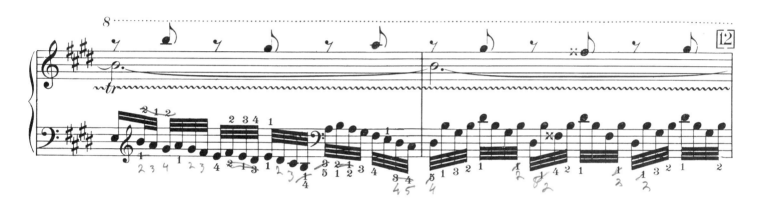

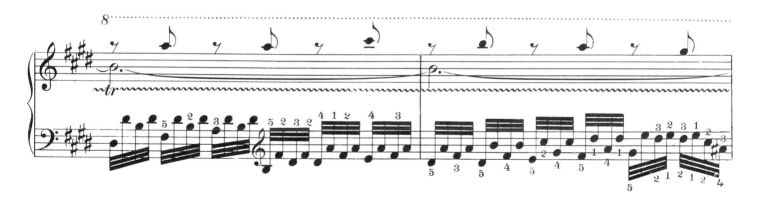

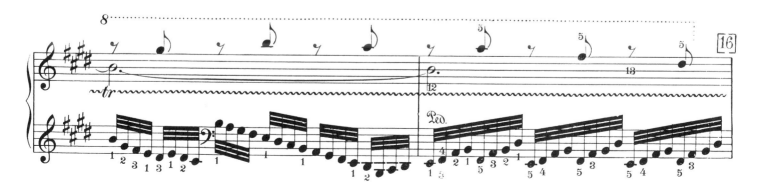

SONATE.

Moderato cantabile molto espressivo.

L. van Beethoven, Op. 110
am 25. Dezember 1821.

31.

*) The fingering in italics and the pedal indications are Beethoven's.

FUGA.
Allegro ma non troppo.

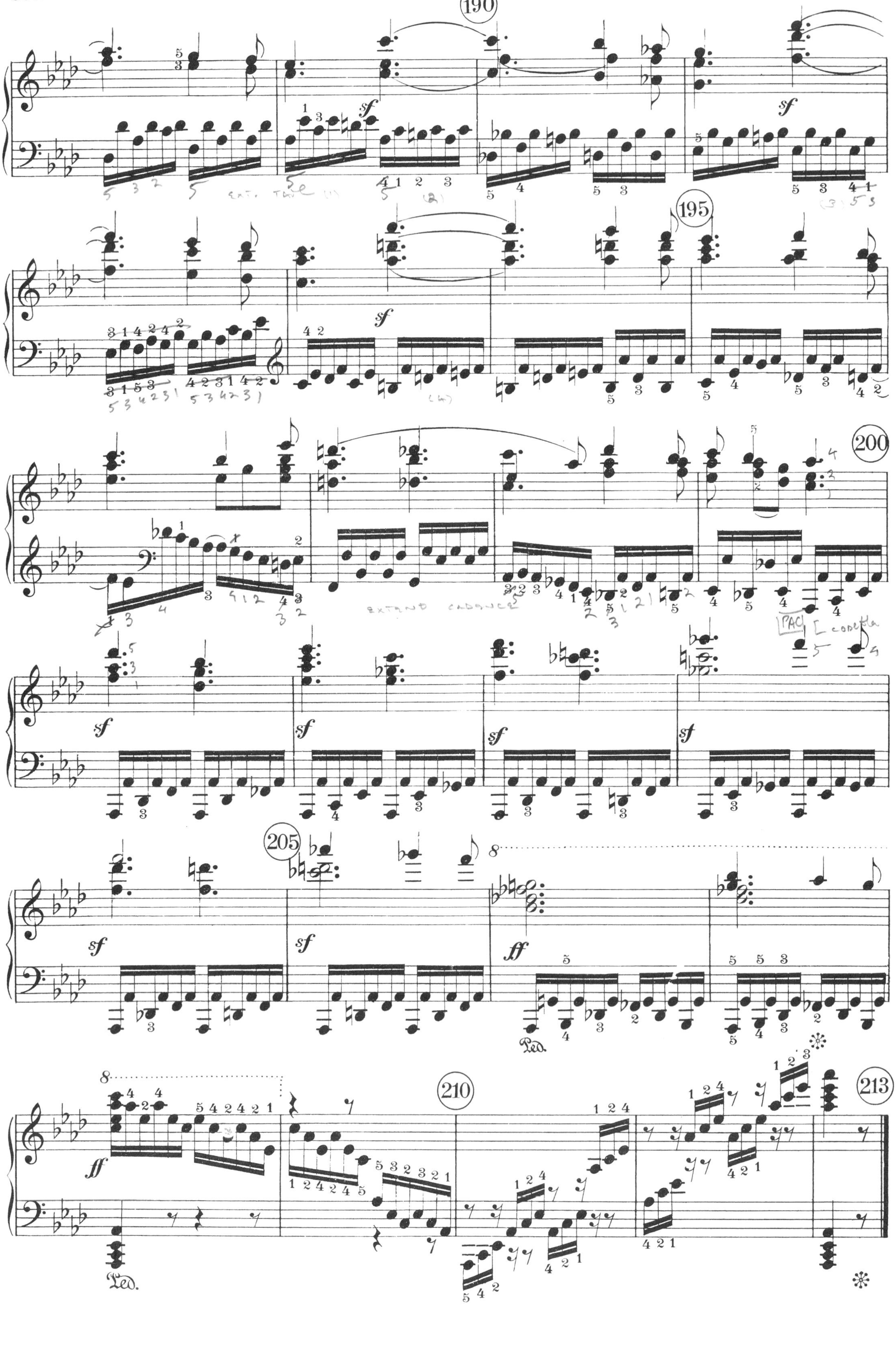
190
195
200
205
210
213
EXTEND CADENCE
PAC
codetta

Sonate.

Dem Erzherzog Rudolph gewidmet.

L. van Beethoven, Op. 111.
Komponiert am 13. Januar 1822.

✳) The fingering in italics and the pedal indications are Beethoven's.

Allegro con brio ed appassionato.

ARIETTA.
Adagio molto semplice e cantabile.

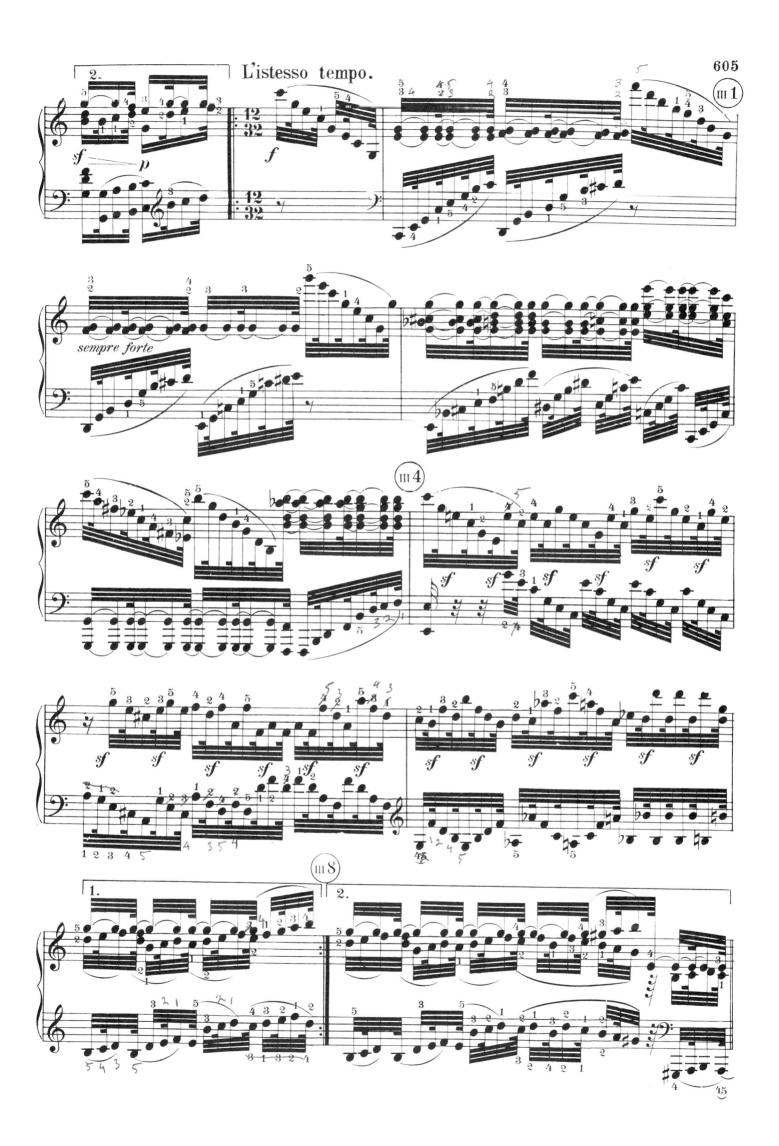

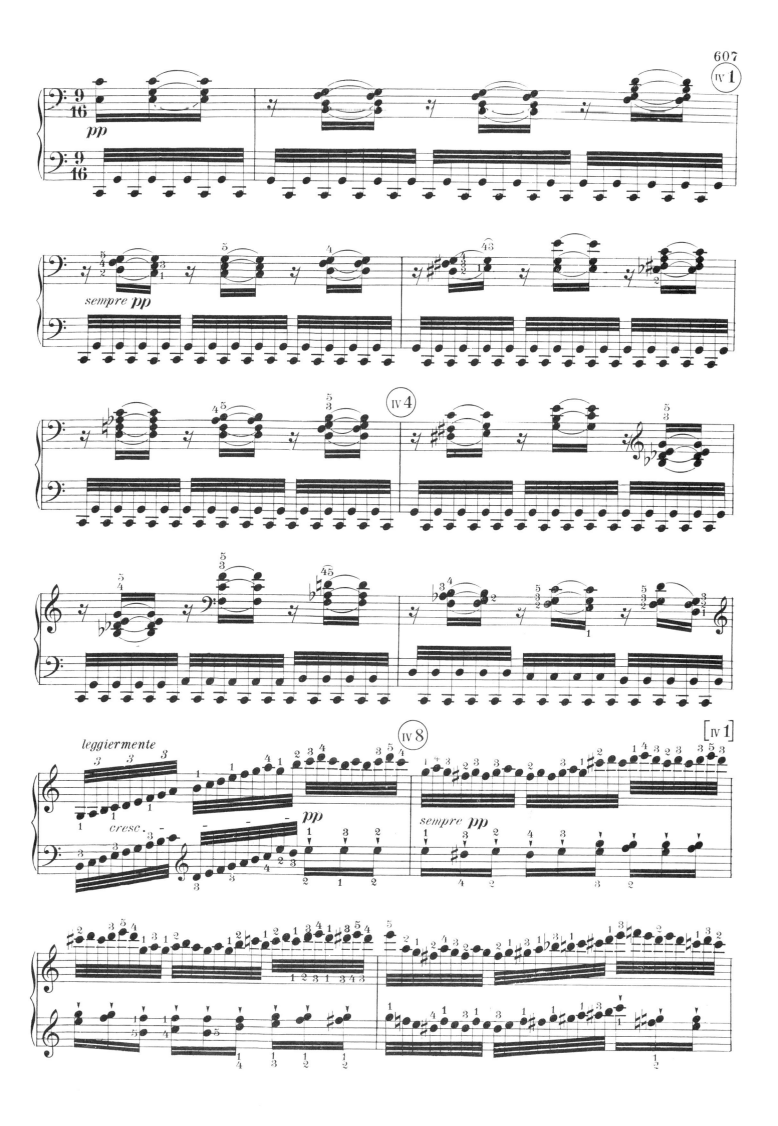

612

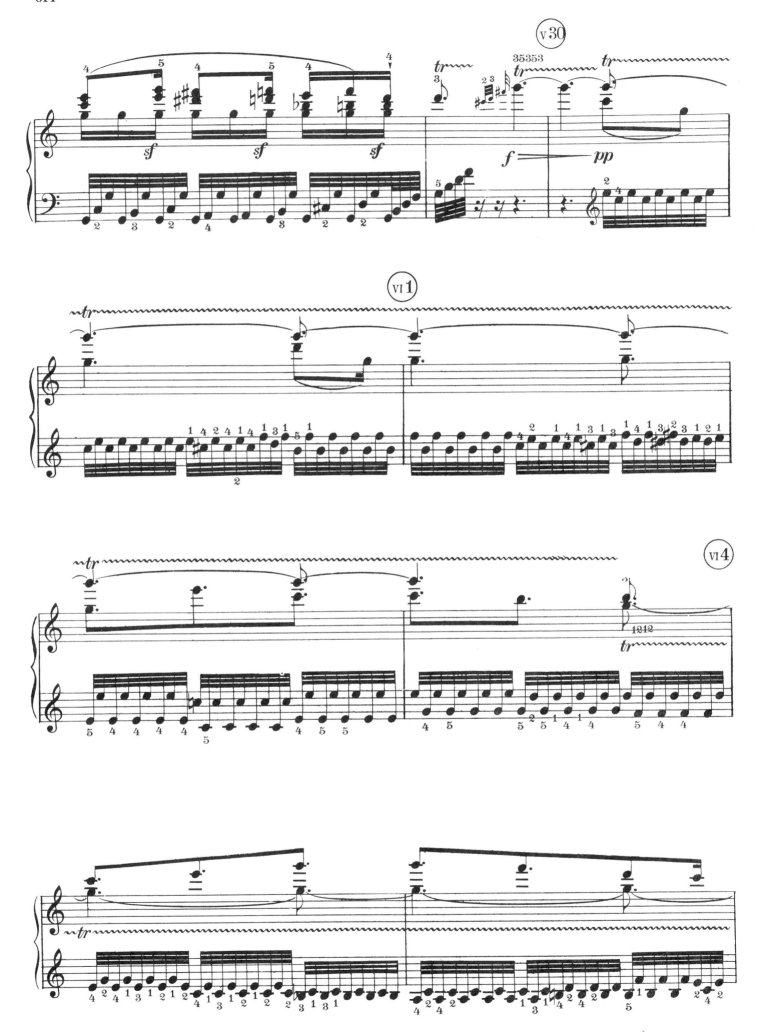

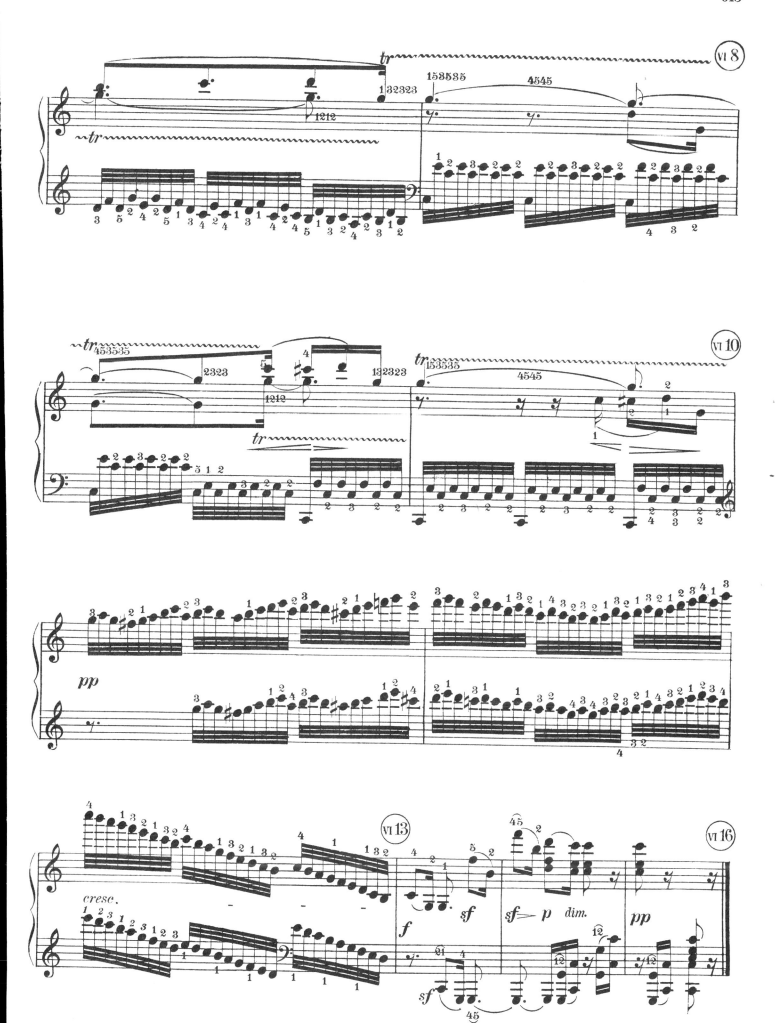